Nail Gun Safety

A Guide for Construction Contractors

Department of Health and Human Services
Centers for Disease Control and Prevention
National Institute for Occupational Safety and Health

Department of Labor
Occupational Safety and Health Administration

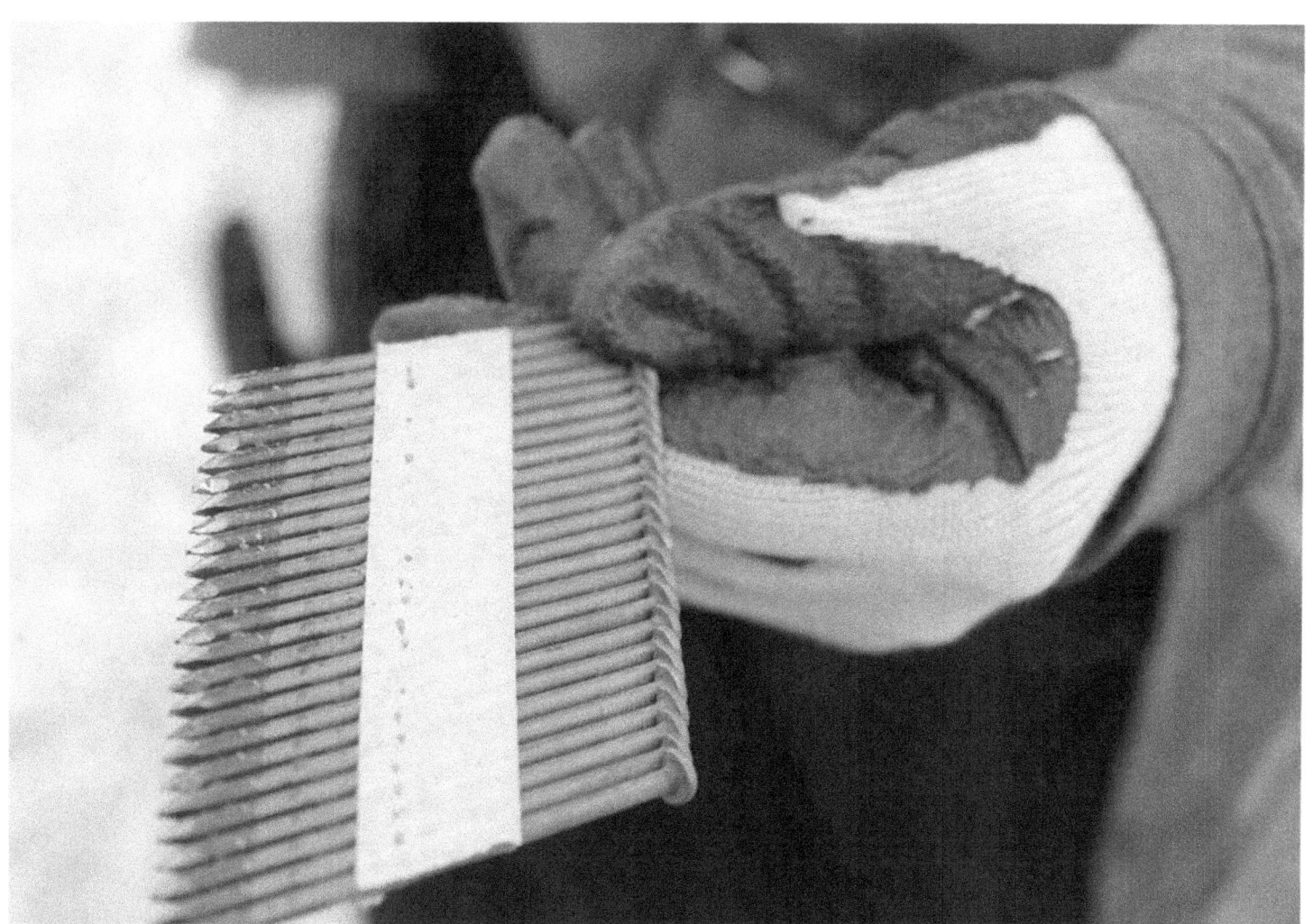

NIOSH and OSHA thank Tom Trauger and Winchester Homes of Bethesda, Maryland
for providing access to residential job sites for photos used in this guidance.

Cover x-ray of a nail gun injury to the hand involving bony penetration requiring
surgical removal. Courtesy of Stephan Mann, MD, MPH; Medical Director, CorpOHS.

Disclaimer

This guidance document is not a standard or regulation, and it creates no new legal obligations. It contains recommendations as well as descriptions of mandatory safety and health standards [and other regulatory requirements]. The recommendations are advisory in nature, informational in content, and are intended to assist employers in providing a safe and healthful workplace. The Occupational Safety and Health Act requires employers to comply with safety and health standards and regulations promulgated by OSHA or by a state with an OSHA-approved state plan. In addition, the Act's General Duty Clause, Section 5(a)(1), requires employers to provide their employees with a workplace free from recognized hazards likely to cause death or serious physical harm.

Ordering Information

Contacting OSHA

To order additional copies of this publication, to get a list of other OSHA publications, to ask questions or to get more information, or to file a confidential complaint, contact OSHA at **1-800-321-OSHA (6742)** or **TTY: 1-877-889-5627** or go to **www.osha.gov.**

Contacting NIOSH

To receive documents or more information about occupational safety and health topics, please contact NIOSH: 1-800-CDC-INFO (1-800-232-4636); TTY: 1-888-232-6348; e-mail: cdcinfo@cdc.gov or visit the NIOSH web site at www.cdc.gov/niosh.

Executive Summary

Nail guns are used every day on many construction jobs—especially in residential construction. They boost productivity but also cause tens of thousands of painful injuries each year. Nail gun injuries are common—one study found that 2 out of 5 residential carpenter apprentices experienced a nail gun injury over a four-year period. When they do occur, these injuries are often not reported or given any medical treatment. Research has identified the risk factors that make nail gun injuries more likely to occur. The type of trigger system and the extent of training are important factors. The risk of a nail gun injury is twice as high when using a multi-shot contact trigger as when using a single-shot sequential trigger nailer.

This guidance is for residential home builders and construction contractors, subcontractors, and supervisors. NIOSH and OSHA developed this publication to give construction employers the information they need to prevent nail gun injuries. Types of triggers and key terms are described. The guidance highlights what is known about nail gun injuries, including the parts of the body most often injured and the types of severe injuries that have been reported. Common causes of nail gun injuries are discussed and six practical steps that contractors can take to prevent these injuries are described. These are:

1) Use full sequential trigger nail guns;
2) Provide training;
3) Establish nail gun work procedures;
4) Provide personal protective equipment (PPE);
5) Encourage reporting and discussion of injuries and close calls; and
6) Provide first aid and medical treatment.

The guidance includes actual workplace cases along with a short section on other types of nail gun hazards and sources of additional information.

Table of Contents

Introduction 1

What the Guidance Covers 1

Know Your Triggers 2

How do Nail Gun Injuries Happen? 4

Six Steps to Nail Gun Safety 6

    1.   Use the full sequential trigger
    2.   Provide training
    3.   Establish nail gun work procedures
    4.   Provide personal protective equipment
    5.   Encourage reporting and discussion of injuries and close calls
    6.   Provide first aid and medical treatment

A Word about Other Hazards 10

Conclusion 11

For Additional Information 12

References and End Notes 13

Introduction

Nail guns are powerful, easy to operate, and boost productivity for nailing tasks. They are also responsible for an estimated 37,000 emergency room visits each year.[1] Severe nail gun injuries have led to construction worker deaths.

Nail gun injuries are common in residential construction. About two-thirds of these injuries occur in framing and sheathing work. Injuries also often occur in roofing and exterior siding and finishing.[2]

How likely are nail gun injuries? A study of apprentice carpenters found that:

- 2 out of 5 were injured using a nail gun during their 4 years of training.
- 1 out of 5 were injured twice.
- 1 out of 10 were injured three or more times.[3]

More than half of reported nail gun injuries are to the hand and fingers.[4] One-quarter of these hand injuries involve structural damage to tendons, joints, nerves, and bones. After hands, the next most often injured are the leg, knee, thigh, foot, and toes. Less common are injuries to the forearm or wrist, head and neck, and trunk. Serious nail gun injuries to the spinal cord, head, neck, eye, internal organs, and bones have been reported. Injuries have resulted in paralysis, blindness, brain damage, bone fractures, and death.

Nail guns present a number of hazards and risks. NIOSH and OSHA prepared this publication to provide builders and contractors with the latest information on nail gun hazards and practical advice on the steps they should take to prevent nail gun injuries on their construction jobs.

What the Guidance Covers

This guide covers nail guns (also called nailers) used for fastening wood, shingles, and siding materials. The guide refers specifically to pneumatic tools but also applies to nail guns that use gas, electric, or hybrid power sources. It does NOT cover powder actuated tools used for fastening material to metal or concrete. The guide assumes that contractors are generally familiar with how nail guns work and the various types of specialized nail guns (for example, framing, roofing, flooring).

This guide is applicable to all nail guns. The emphasis is on framing ("stick" and "coil") nail guns because they fire the largest nails, are the most powerful, and are considered to be the most dangerous to use.

Worksite Story

A 26-year-old Idaho construction worker died following a nail gun accident in April 2007. He was framing a house when he slipped and fell. His finger was on the contact trigger of the nail gun he was using. The nosepiece hit his head as he fell, driving a 3-inch nail into his skull. The nail injured his brain stem, causing his death. The safety controls on the nail gun were found to be intact. Death and serious injury can occur using nail guns—even when they are working properly.

Know Your Triggers

Nail gun safety starts with understanding the various trigger mechanisms. Here is what you need to know:

How triggers differ

All nailers rely on two basic controls: a finger trigger and a contact safety tip located on the nose of the gun. Trigger mechanisms can vary based on: 1) the order in which the controls are activated, and 2) whether the trigger can be held in the squeezed position to discharge multiple nails OR if it must be released and then squeezed again for each individual nail. Combining these variations gives four kinds of triggers. Some nail guns have a selective trigger switch which allows the user to choose among two or more trigger systems. Each trigger type is described below along with a summary of how the controls are activated.

Full Sequential trigger

This is the safest type of nail gun trigger. This trigger will only fire a nail when the controls are activated in a certain order. First, the safety contact tip must be pushed into the work piece, then the user squeezes the trigger to discharge a nail. Both the safety contact tip and the trigger must be released and activated again to fire a second nail. Nails cannot be bump fired. Also known as single-shot trigger, restrictive trigger, or trigger fire mode.

Single nail:
Push safety contact, then squeeze trigger

Multiple nails:
Release both safety contact and trigger and repeat process

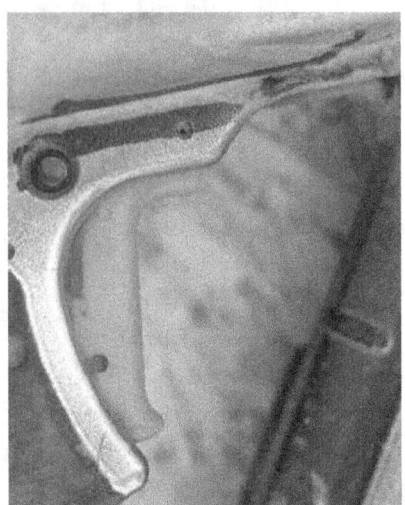

Trigger

Contact safety tip

Contact trigger

Fires a nail when the safety contact and trigger are activated in any order. You can push the safety contact tip first and then squeeze the trigger, or you can squeeze the trigger first and then push the safety contact tip. If the trigger is kept squeezed, a nail will be driven each time the safety contact is pushed in. All nails can be bump fired. Also known as bump trigger, multi-shot trigger, successive trigger, dual-action, touch trip, contact trip, and bottom fire.

Single nail:
Push safety contact, then squeeze trigger, or squeeze trigger, then push safety contact

Multiple nails:
Squeeze and hold trigger, then push safety contact to fire one nail, move and push safety contact again to fire additional nails

Bump firing or bounce nailing is using a nail gun with a contact trigger held squeezed and bumping or bouncing the tool along the work piece to fire nails. Red dots show path of motion.

Single Sequential trigger

Like the full sequential trigger, this trigger will only fire a nail when the controls are activated in a certain order. First, the safety contact tip must be pushed into the work piece. Then, the user squeezes the trigger to discharge a nail. To fire a second nail, only the trigger must be released. The safety contact tip can stay pressed into the work piece. Nails cannot be bump fired.

Single nail:
Push safety contact, then squeeze trigger

Multiple nails:
Release trigger, move tool, and squeeze trigger to fire additional nail

Single Actuation trigger

Like the contact trigger, this trigger will fire a single nail when the safety contact and trigger are activated in any order. A second nail can be fired by releasing the trigger, moving the tool and squeezing the trigger again without releasing the safety contact tip. Note that some manufacturers refer to these triggers as "single sequential triggers", but they are different. The first nail can be bump fired with a single actuation trigger but not with a true single sequential trigger.

Single nail:
Push safety contact, squeeze trigger, or squeeze trigger, then push safety contact to fire

Multiple nails:
Release trigger, move tool, and squeeze trigger to fire additional nail

Other trigger terms

The International Staple, Nail and Tool Association (ISANTA) voluntary standard includes technical definitions for trigger "actuation systems". Tool manufacturers have names for trigger modes such as "intermittent operation method" or "precision placement driving". Contractors and workers use their own names for triggers and operating modes such as "single shot" and "multi-shot".

The bottom line: contractors should check the tool label and manual for manufacturer-specific trigger names and operating information.

How do Nail Gun Injuries Happen?

Useful terms

Recoil is the rapid rebound or kick-back after the nailer is fired.

A double fire occurs when a second nail unintentionally fires because the nailer re-contacted the work piece after recoil. It can also occur if the safety contact slips while the user is positioning the nail gun. Several tool manufacturers offer "anti-double fire" features for their nail guns.

You should know

Unintended nail discharge is a common source of injuries. A study of workers' compensation records found that two-thirds of nail gun injury claims involved some type of unintended nail gun discharge or misfire.[6]

Worksite Story

Two framers were working together to lay down and nail a subfloor. One framer was waiting and holding the nail gun with his finger on the contact trigger. The other framer was walking backwards toward him and dragging a sheet of plywood. The framer handling the plywood backed into the tip of the nail gun and was shot in the back. The nail nicked his kidney, but fortunately he recovered. As a result of this incident, the contractor switched to using only sequential triggers on framing nail guns. Co-workers can get injured if they bump into your contact trigger nail gun. You can prevent this by using a full sequential trigger.

There are seven major risk factors that can lead to a nail gun injury. Understanding them will help you to prevent injuries on your jobsites.

Unintended nail discharge from double fire.
Occurs with CONTACT triggers.

The Consumer Product Safety Commission (CPSC) found that contact trigger nailers are susceptible to double firing, especially when trying to accurately place the nailer against the work piece.[5] They found that a second unintended firing can happen faster than the user is able to react and release the trigger. Unintended nails can cause injuries.

Double fire can be a particular problem for new workers who may push hard on the tool to compensate for recoil. It can also occur when the user is working in an awkward position, such as in tight spaces where the gun doesn't have enough space to recoil. The recoil of the gun itself can even cause a non-nail injury in tight spaces if the nail gun hits the user's head or face.

Unintended nail discharge from knocking the safety contact with the trigger squeezed.
Occurs with CONTACT and SINGLE ACTUATION triggers.

Nail guns with contact and single actuation triggers will fire if the trigger is being held squeezed and the safety contact tip gets knocked or pushed into an object or person by mistake. For example, a framer might knock his leg going down a ladder or bump into a co-worker passing through a doorway. Contact trigger nailers can release multiple nails and single actuation trigger nailers can release a single nail to cause injury.

Holding or carrying contact trigger or single actuation trigger nail guns with the trigger squeezed increases the risk of unintended nail discharge. Construction workers tend to keep a finger on the trigger because it is more natural to hold and carry an 8-pound nail gun using a full, four-finger grip. Tool manufacturers, however, do warn against it.

Nail penetration through lumber work piece.
Occurs with ALL trigger types.

Nails can pass through a work piece and either hit the worker's hand or fly off as a projectile (airborne) nail. A blow-out nail is one example. Blow-outs can occur when a nail is placed near a knot in the wood. Knots involve a change in wood grain, which creates both weak spots and hard spots that can make the nail change direction and exit the work piece. Nail penetration is especially a concern for placement work where a piece of lumber needs to be held in place by hand. If the nail misses or breaks through the lumber it can injure the non-dominant hand holding it.

Nail ricochet after striking a hard surface or metal feature.

Occurs with ALL trigger types.

When a nail hits a hard surface, it has to change direction and it can bounce off the surface, becoming a projectile. Wood knots and metal framing hardware are common causes of ricochets. Problems have also been noted with ricochets when nailing into dense laminated beams. Ricochet nails can strike the worker or a co-worker to cause an injury.

Missing the work piece.

Occurs with ALL trigger types.

Injuries may occur when the tip of the nail gun does not make full contact with the work piece and the discharged nail becomes airborne. This can occur when nailing near the edge of a work piece, such as a plate. Positioning the safety contact is more difficult in these situations and sometimes the fired nail completely misses the lumber. Injuries have also occurred when a nail shot through plywood or oriented strand board sheeting missed a stud and became airborne.

Awkward position nailing.

Occurs with ALL trigger types.

Unintended discharges are a concern in awkward position work with CONTACT and SINGLE ACTUATION triggers.

Nailing in awkward positions where the tool and its recoil are more difficult to control may increase the risk of injury. These include toe-nailing, nailing above shoulder height, nailing in tight quarters, holding the nail gun with the non-dominant hand, nailing while on a ladder, or nailing when the user's body is in the line of fire (nailing towards yourself). Toe-nailing is awkward because the gun cannot be held flush against the work piece. Nailing from a ladder makes it difficult to position the nail gun accurately. Nailing beyond a comfortable reach distance from a ladder, elevated work platform, or leading edge also places the user at risk for a fall.

Bypassing safety mechanisms.

Occurs with ALL trigger types.

Bypassing or disabling certain features of either the trigger or safety contact tip is an important risk of injury. For example, removing the spring from the safety contact tip makes an unintended discharge even more likely. Modifying tools can lead to safety problems for anyone who uses the nail gun. Nail gun manufacturers strongly recommend against bypassing safety features, and voluntary standards prohibit modifications or tampering.[7] OSHA's Construction standard at 29 CFR 1926.300(a) requires that all hand and power tools and similar equipment, whether furnished by the employer or the employee shall be maintained in a safe condition.

Common nail gun grip with finger on trigger

Nail penetration through the lumber is a special concern where the piece is held in place by hand

Toe -nailing

Studies of residential carpenters found that the overall risk of nail gun injury is twice as high when using contact trigger nail guns compared to using sequential trigger nail guns.[8]

Note that the studies could not quantify injury risks associated with specific tasks; it is likely that some nailing tasks are more dangerous than others.

About 1 in 10 nail gun injuries happen to co-workers.[9] This is from either airborne (projectile) nails or bumping into a co-worker while carrying a contact trigger nail gun with the trigger squeezed.

A voluntary ANSI standard[10] calls for all large pneumatic framing nailers manufactured after 2003 to be shipped with a sequential trigger. However, these may not always be FULL SEQUENTIAL triggers. Contractors may need to contact manufacturers or suppliers to purchase a FULL SEQUENTIAL trigger kit.

Worksite story

A carpenter apprentice on his first day ever using a nail gun injured his right leg. He was working on a step ladder and was in the process of lowering the nail gun to his side when the gun struck his leg and fired a nail into it. He had no training prior to using the nail gun. New worker training is important and should include hands-on skills.

Six Steps to Nail Gun Safety

❶ Use the full sequential trigger

The full sequential trigger is always the safest trigger mechanism for the job. It reduces the risk of unintentional nail discharge and double fires—including injuries from bumping into co-workers.

- At a minimum, provide full sequential trigger nailers for placement work where the lumber needs to be held in place by hand. Examples include building walls and nailing blocking, fastening studs to plates and blocks to studs, and installing trusses.

  Unintended nail discharge is more likely to lead to a hand or arm injury for placement work compared to flat work, where the lumber does not need to be held in place by hand. Examples of flat work include roofing, sheathing, and subflooring.

- Consider restricting inexperienced employees to full sequential trigger nail guns starting out. Some contractors using more than one type of trigger on their jobs color-code the nail guns so that the type of trigger can be readily identified by workers and supervisors.

- Some contractors have been reluctant to use full sequential triggers fearing a loss of productivity. How do the different types of triggers compare?

  The one available study had 10 experienced framers stick-build two identical small (8 ft x 10 ft) wood structures—one using a sequential trigger nail gun and one using a contact trigger nail gun. Small structures were built in this study so that there would be time for each carpenter to complete two sheds.

  Average nailing time using the contact trigger was 10% faster, which accounted for less than 1% of the total building time when cutting and layout was included.[11] However, in this study the trigger type was less important to overall productivity than who was using the tool; this suggests productivity concerns should focus on the skill of the carpenter rather than on the trigger.

  Although the study did not evaluate framing a residence or light commercial building, it shows that productivity is not just about the trigger. The wood structures built for the study did include common types of nailing tasks (flat nailing, through nailing, toe-nailing) and allowed comparisons for both total average nailing time and overall project time. The study did not compare productivity differences for each type of nailing task used to build the sheds.

❷ Provide training

Both new and experienced workers can benefit from safety training to learn about the causes of nail gun injuries and specific steps to reduce them. Be sure that training is provided in a manner that employees can understand. Here is a list of topics for training:

- How nail guns work and how triggers differ.

- Main causes of injuries – especially differences among types of triggers.

- Instructions provided in manufacturer tool manuals and where the manual is kept.

- Hands-on training with the actual nailers to be used on the job. This gives each employee an opportunity to handle the nailer and to get feedback on topics such as:

  - How to load the nail gun

  - How to operate the air compressor

  - How to fire the nail gun

  - How to hold lumber during placement work

  - How to recognize and approach ricochet-prone work surfaces

  - How to handle awkward position work (e.g., toe-nailing and work on ladders)

  - How best to handle special risks associated with contact and single actuation triggers such as nail gun recoil and double fires. For example, coach new employees on how to minimize double fires by allowing the nail gun to recoil rather than continuing to push against the gun after it fires.

- What to do when a nail gun malfunctions.

- Training should also cover items covered in the following sections of the guidance, such as company nail gun work procedures, personal protective equipment, injury reporting, and first aid and medical treatment.

❸ Establish nail gun work procedures

Contractors should develop their own nail gun work rules and procedures to address risk factors and make the work as safe as possible. Examples of topics for contractor work procedures include but are not limited to the following:

Do's...

- Make sure that tool manuals for the nailers used on the job are always available on the jobsite.

- Make sure that manufacturers' tool labels and instructions are understood and followed.

- Check tools and power sources before operating to make sure that they are in proper working order. Take broken or malfunctioning nail guns out of service immediately.

Worksite story

After his crews experienced many double fires and a related serious nail gun injury, a New Jersey contractor switched to using only sequential triggers. He believes he has eliminated the risk of double fire injuries and he estimates that the change has had only a slight impact on productivity—a few extra hours per house.

You should know

Training is important: untrained workers are more likely to experience a nail gun injury than a trained worker. [12]

Training does not trump triggers: trained workers using contact triggers still have twice the overall risk of injury as trained workers using sequential triggers.

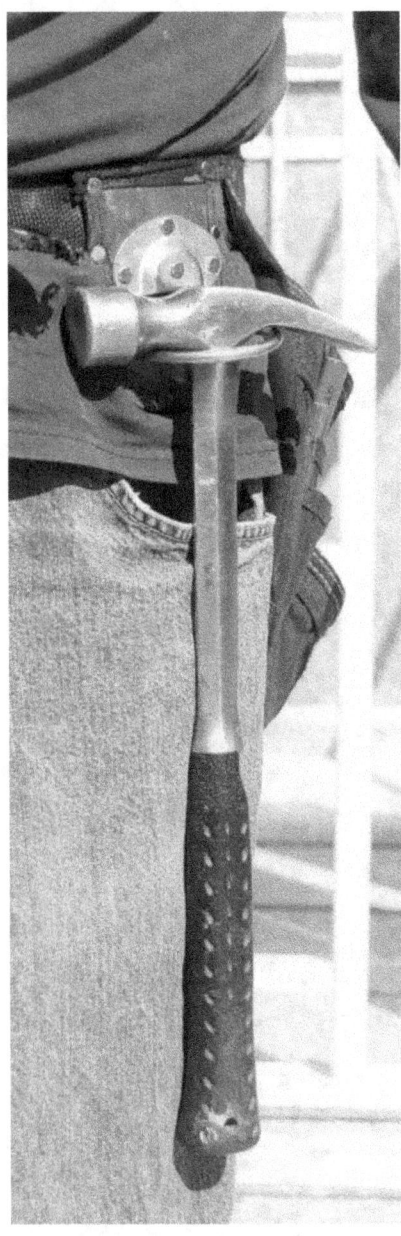

- Set up operations so that workers are not in the line of fire from nail guns being operated by co-workers.

- Check lumber surfaces before nailing. Look for knots, nails, straps, hangers, etc. that could cause recoil or ricochet.

- Use a hammer or positive placement nailer when nailing metal joinery or irregular lumber.

- For placement work, keep hands at least 12 inches away from the nailing point at all times. Consider using clamps to brace instead of your hands.

- Always shoot nail guns away from your body and away from co-workers.

- Always disconnect the compressed air when:

  - Leaving a nailer unattended;

  - Travelling up and down a ladder or stairs;

  - Passing the nail gun to a co-worker;

  - Clearing jammed nails;

  - Performing any other maintenance on the nail gun.

- Recognize the dangers of awkward position work and provide extra time and precautions:

  - Use a hammer if you cannot reach the work while holding the nailer with your dominant hand.

  - Use a hammer or reposition for work at face or head height. Recoil is more difficult to control and could be dangerous.

  - Use a hammer or full sequential trigger nailer when working in a tight space. Recoil is more difficult to control and double fires could occur with contact triggers.

  - Take extra care with toe-nailing. Nail guns can slip before or during firing because the gun cannot be held flush against the work piece. Use a nail gun with teeth on the safety contact to bite into the work piece to keep the gun from slipping during the shot. Use the trigger to fire only after the safety contact piece is positioned.

- Recognize the dangers of nail gun work at height and provide extra time and precautions:

  - Set up jobs to minimize the need for nailing at height.

  - Consider using scaffolds instead of ladders.

  - If work must be done on ladders, use full sequential trigger nailers to prevent nail gun injuries which could occur from bumping a leg while climbing up or down a ladder.

  - Position ladders so you don't have to reach too far. Your belt buckle should stay between the side rails when reaching to the side.

- Maintain three points of contact with the ladder at all times to prevent a fall—this means that clamps may need to be used for placement work. Holding a nailer in one hand and the work piece with the other provides only two points of contact (your feet). Reaching and recoil can make you lose your balance and fall. Falls, especially with contact trigger nailers, can result in nail gun injuries.

Don'ts...

- Never bypass or disable nail gun safety features. This is strictly prohibited. Tampering includes removing the spring from the safety-contact tip and/or tying down, taping or otherwise securing the trigger so it does not need to be pressed. Tampering increases the chance that the nail gun will fire unintentionally both for the current user and anyone else who may use the nail gun. Nail gun manufacturers strongly recommend against tampering and OSHA requires that tools be maintained in a safe condition. There is NO legitimate reason to modify or disable a nail gun safety device.

- Encourage your workers to keep their fingers off the trigger when holding or carrying a nail gun. If this is not natural, workers should use a full sequential nail gun or set down the nailer until they begin to nail again.

- Never lower the nail gun from above or drag the tool by the hose. If the nail-gun hose gets caught on something, don't pull on the hose. Go find the problem and release the hose.

- Never use the nailer with the non-dominant hand.

❹ Provide Personal Protective Equipment (PPE)

Safety shoes, which help protect workers' toes from nail gun injuries, are typically required by OSHA on residential construction sites. In addition, employers should provide, at no cost to employees, the following protective equipment for workers using nail guns:

- Hard hats
- High Impact eye protection – safety glasses or goggles marked ANSI Z87.1
- Hearing protection – either earplugs or earmuffs

❺ Encourage reporting and discussion of injuries and close calls

Studies show that many nail gun injuries go unreported. Employers should ensure that their policies and practices encourage reporting of nail gun injuries. Reporting helps ensure that employees get medical attention (see #6 below). It also helps contractors to identify unrecognized job site risks that could lead to additional injuries if not addressed. Injuries and close calls provide teachable moments that can help improve crew safety.

If you have a safety incentive program, be sure that it does not discourage workers from reporting injuries. Employers that intentionally underreport work-related injuries will be in violation of OSHA's injury and illness recordkeeping regulation.

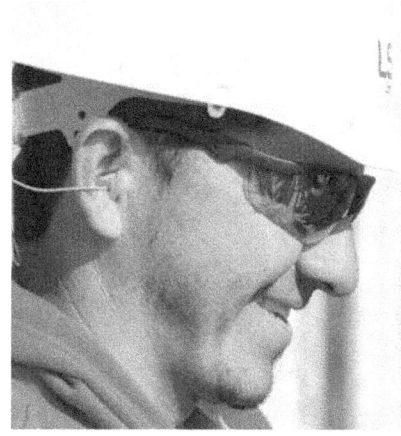

Worker using recommended PPE when working with nail guns: hard hat, safety glasses, and hearing protection

A construction worker accidentally drove a 16 penny framing nail into his thigh. It didn't bleed much and he didn't seek medical care. He removed the nail himself. Three days later he felt a snap in his leg and severe pain. In the emergency room, doctors removed a sheared off nail and found that his thigh bone had fractured. Not all injuries are immediately visible. Failure to seek medical care can result in complications and more serious injuries.

⑥ Provide first aid and medical treatment

Employers and workers should seek medical attention immediately after nail gun injuries, even for hand injuries that appear to be minimal. Studies suggest that 1 out of 4 nail gun hand injuries can involve some type of structural damage such as bone fracture.[13] Materials such as nail strip glue or plastic or even clothing can get embedded in the injury and lead to infection. Barbs on the nail can cause secondary injury if the nail is removed incorrectly. These complications can be avoided by having workers seek immediate medical care.

A Word about Other Hazards

Air pressure. Pneumatic tools and compressor use are regulated under OSHA's Construction standard at 29 CFR 1926.302(b). The provisions in this standard that are relevant for nail guns are provided below.

(1) Pneumatic power tools shall be secured to the hose or whip by some positive means to prevent the tool from becoming accidentally disconnected.

Note: An OSHA letter of interpretation[14] allows the use of a quick disconnect with a pull-down sleeve to meet this requirement. It is composed of a male fitting (connector) and female fitting (coupling) that has a sleeve which must be pulled away from the end of the hose to separate the two fittings to prevent the tool from becoming accidentally disconnected.

(3) All pneumatically driven nailers, staplers, and other similar equipment provided with automatic fastener feed, which operate at more than 100 p.s.i. pressure at the tool shall have a safety device on the muzzle to prevent the tool from ejecting fasteners, unless the muzzle is in contact with the work surface.

(5) The manufacturer's safe operating pressure for hoses, pipes, valves, filters, and other fittings shall not be exceeded.

(6) The use of hoses for hoisting or lowering tools shall not be permitted.

Noise. Pneumatic nail guns produce short (less than a tenth of a second in duration) but loud "impulse" noise peaks: one from driving the nail and one from exhausting the air. Most nail gun manufacturers recommend that users wear hearing protection when operating a nailer.

Available information indicates that nail gun noise can vary depending on the gun, the work piece, air pressure, and the work setting. The type of trigger system does not appear to affect the noise level. Peak noise emission levels for several nailers ranged from 109 to 136 dBA.[15,16] These loud short bursts can contribute to hearing loss. Employers should provide hearing protection in the form of earplugs or muffs and ensure that they are worn correctly. Employers should also ask about noise levels when buying nail guns—studies have identified ways to reduce nail gun noise and some manufacturers may incorporate noise reduction features.

Note: OSHA's standard for exposure to continuous noise levels (29 CFR 1926.52) addresses both the noise level and the duration of exposure. In this standard, workers exposed for 15 minutes at 115 A-weighted decibels (dBA) have the same exposure as workers exposed for 8 hours at 90 dBA.

The NIOSH and OSHA limit for impulse noise is 140 decibels: above this level a single exposure can cause instant damage to the ear.

NIOSH recommends that an 8-hour exposure should not exceed 85 dBA and a one-second exposure should not exceed 130 dBA without using hearing protection.

Musculoskeletal disorders. Framing nail guns can weigh up to 8 pounds and many framing jobs require workers to hold and use these guns for long periods of time in awkward hand/arm postures. Holding an 8-pound weight for long periods of time can lead to musculoskeletal symptoms such as soreness or tenderness in the fingers, wrist, or forearm tendons or muscles. These symptoms can progress to pain, or in the most severe cases, inability to work. No studies have shown that one trigger type is any more or less likely to cause musculoskeletal problems from long periods of nail gun use. If use of a nail gun is causing musculoskeletal pain or symptoms of musculoskeletal disorders, medical care should be sought.

Conclusion

Nail gun injuries are painful. Some cause severe injuries or death. Nail gun injuries have been on the rise along with the increased popularity of these powerful tools. These injuries can be prevented, and more and more contractors are making changes to improve nail gun safety. Take a look at your practices and use this guide to improve safety on your job sites. Working together with tool gun manufacturers, safety and health professionals, and other organizations, we can reduce nail gun injuries.

For Additional Information

OSHA
Woodworking eTool—Handheld Nail/Stapling Guns
www.osha.gov/SLTC/etools/woodworking/production_handheldstaplegun.html

Center for Construction Research and Training (CPWR)
Nail Gun Hazard Alert
www.cpwr.com/hazpdfs/Nail%20Gun%20Safety%202pg%20flier%20FINAL.pdf
Nail Gun Injuries, Productivity, and Recommendations
www.elcosh.org/en/document/1160/d001056/nail-guns%253A-injuries%252C-productivity-and-recommendations.html

International Staple, Nail and Tool Association (ISANTA)
American National Standard SNT-101-2002—Safety Requirements for Portable, Compressed-Air-Actuated
Fastener Driving Tools.
Home Page www.isanta.org/

Oregon OSHA
Pneumatic Nail and Staple Gun Safety Hazard Alert
www.orosha.org/pdf/hazards/2993-21.pdf

California OSHA
Pneumatically Driven Nailers and Staplers CCR Title 8, Section 1704
www.dir.ca.gov/Title8/1704.html

Nail gun video materials
WorkSafe British Columbia—Nail Gun Safety, and Safe Handling of Nail Guns
www2.worksafebc.com/Publications/Multimedia/Videos.asp?ReportID=35773

Unsafe Handling of Nail Guns. Case study and video
www.speakingofsafety.ca/2011/04/28/unsafe-handling-of-nail-guns/

Sacramento Bee—Nail Gun Safety
www.youtube.com/watch?v=MsCu9luSRRY&feature=related

References and Endnotes

[1] 68% of these emergency room visits involved workers and 32% involved consumers. From: Lipscomb H, Jackson L [2007]. Nail-Gun Injuries treated in Emergency Departments—United States, 2001-2005. MMWR 56(14):329-332.

[2] Dement J, Lipscomb H, Leiming L, Epling C, Desai, T [2003]. Nail Gun Injuries among Construction Workers. Appl Occup Environ Hyg 18(5):374-383.

[3] Lipscomb H, Dement J, Nolan J, Patterson D. [2006]. Nail Gun Injuries in Apprentice Carpenters: Risk Factors and Control Measures. Am J Ind Med 49:505-513.

[4] Lipscomb H, Nolan J, Patterson D, Dement D [2010]. Surveillance of Nail Gun Injuries by Journeyman Carpenters provides important Insight into Experiences of Apprentices. New Solutions 20(1) 95-114. Also, Baggs J, Cohen M, Kalat J, Silverstein, B [2001]. Pneumatic Nailer Injuries—A Report on Washington State 1990-1998. Prof Saf Mag January: 3V-38.

[5] Consumer Products Safety Commission (CPSC), [2002]. Evaluation of Pneumatic Nailers. Memo from Carolene Paul to Jacqueline Elder. May 23, 2002. See http://www.cpsc.gov/library/foia/foia02/os/nailers.pdf.

[6] Dement J, Lipscomb H, Leiming L, Epling C, Desai, T [2003]. Nail Gun Injuries among Construction Workers. Appl Occup Environ Hyg 18(5):374-383.

[7] American National Standard Institute (ANSI) [2002]. Safety Requirements for Portable, Compressed-Air-Actuated Fastener Driving Tools. ANSI SNT-101-2002 Sections 4.4: Tools shall not be modified or altered; 8.4.2.3: Improperly functioning tools must not be used; 8.4.2.5.1: Do not remove, tamper with, or otherwise cause the tool operating controls to become inoperable.

[8] Lipscomb H, Nolan J, Patterson D, Dement D [2010]. Surveillance of Nail Gun Injuries by Journeyman Carpenters provides important Insight into Experiences of Apprentices. New Solutions 20(1) 95-114. Also Lipscomb H, Nolan J, Patterson D, Dement J [2008]. Prevention of Traumatic Nail Gun Injuries in Apprentice Carpenters: Use of Population-Based Measures to Monitor Intervention Effectiveness. Am J Ind Med 51:719-727.

[9] See Footnote 8.

[10] See Footnote 7. See Section 4.1.3.

[11] Lipscomb H, Nolan J, Patterson D, Makrozahopoulos D, Kucera K, Dement J [2008]. How Much Time is Safety Worth? A Comparison of Trigger Configurations on Pneumatic Nail Guns in Residential Framing. Public Health Reports 123:481-486.

[12] See Footnote 3.

[13] Hussey K, Knox D, Lambah A, Curnier A, Holmes J, Davies, M [2008]. Nail Gun Injuries to the Hand. Trauma 64:1:170-173.

[14] See http://www.osha.gov/pls/oshaweb/owadisp.show_document?p_table=INTERPRETATIONS&p_id=24786.

[15] Health and Safety Executive [2008]. Noise Emissions from Fastener Driving Tools. Research Report 625.

[16] Malkin et al. [2005] An Assessment of Occupational Safety and Health Hazards in Selected Small Business Manufacturing Wood Pallets—Part 1. Noise and Physical Hazards. J. Occ. Env. Hyg. 2: D18-21.

[17] See NIOSH-sponsored student engineering studies evaluated nail gun noise and noise reduction options at http://www.cdc.gov/niosh/topics/noise/collegestudents/pneumaticnailgun.html.

www.ingramcontent.com/pod-product-compliance
Lightning Source LLC
Chambersburg PA
CBHW081423170526
45166CB00010B/3443

*9 7 8 1 4 7 8 1 6 2 9 0 2 *